WHAT TO DO WHEN YOU'RE

73

FINANCIAL CONSIDERATIONS
FOR LIFE'S STAGES
3rd Edition

JAMES J. MILLINGTON

authorHOUSE®

AuthorHouse™
1663 Liberty Drive
Bloomington, IN 47403
www.authorhouse.com
Phone: 833-262-8899

Published by AuthorHouse 03/22/2023

ISBN: 978-1-6655-1624-2 (sc)
ISBN: 978-1-6655-1625-9 (e)

Library of Congress Control Number: 2021902488

I've spent close to 25 years in the financial services industry and a lot of our financial decisions are based on where we are in life, what age we've attained or by other deadlines such as tax-day. A lot of times, people arrive at a certain age, and it prompts them to think of different matters, such as getting a new job, getting married, starting a family, thinking about retirement, retiring, or having a realization of the finality of life. On the other hand, many times, laws allow us to either be able to do or not do things based on our age. This book is designed to capture both the life-stage planning that should be considered at certain ages in addition to what the rules allow for or force upon one-self.

AGE 0 BIRTH — STARTING TO SAVE

You're born! Since you, that have just been born, are not reading this but perhaps your parents are reading this and they are wondering what they can do for you now. When you're born, you get your social security number, which is the key to opening new accounts. Most parents want to know, which account should be opened for kids. Well, it depends on the goal. Generally, it winds down to college or general savings.

The college savings account, called a 529 Savings Plan, is probably the best account to use to save for college. Every state sponsors their own plan and they work with one or two financial companies to provide the accounts. Benefits are many, including tax savings and financial aid. The funds can be used for educational expenses including in some instances room and board. The account has some restrictions as to when you can take the money out and what college expenses it can be used for. Therefore, the goal truly should be college related. Most plans allow you to open with a small deposit and add money on a recurring basis or contribute as you have it. The investment options tend to be mutual funds but it works for a wide range of savers. The 529 college savings account can now be used for tuition from K through 12th grade for up to $10,000 of expenses.

The other type of college savings account is a Coverdell Education Savings account. The Education Savings account works like an IRA because it has a maximum yearly contribution which is $2,000. The benefit of the accounts is that it can be used for college or K through 12 expenses as well, but you can also invest in a wider variety of options such as stocks, bonds, or mutual funds that might not be available in the 529 college savings plan.

Another type of arrangement is called a Prepaid Tuition Plan. Some states offer this type of savings program and essentially, you're paying the future cost of school but at today's prices so you are locking in the cost. The funds are tax free if used for college tuition. However, the limitation to these plans is that they typically only cover tuition costs. Room and board are not eligible costs. They are usually allowed for certain institutions. If the funds are not used for school, the money can be returned but without any appreciation.

The other option would be a custodian account. A custodian account can be opened at a bank or investment company. Essentially, it is an account in the child's name and someone is the custodian, typically the parent or grandparent. This doesn't have the restrictions like the other accounts such as having to be used for school expenses, however it doesn't offer the tax and financial aid benefits. This account would be used for other things for the child. The money is an irrevocable gift, so the money in the account is legally the minors. Once the child turns the age of majority, usually 18 or 21, depending on the state where the account was opened in, the money is now the child's.

AGE 14 WORKING AGE — START SAVING FOR CHILD

Really at any age, a parent can open an IRA for a child to save for later in life. If the child has earned income, the parent can contribute the earned income of the child up to $6,500 per year. Just like an adult, if the earned income is $1,000, then the maximum contribution is $1,000. Both a traditional and Roth IRA can be opened for a child. Remember the Traditional IRA allows for the contribution to be deducted off your taxes which reduces this year's gross income. The Roth IRA doesn't allow for a deduction from yearly income, however it will grow tax free for life while within the Roth IRA. The Traditional IRA will be taxed upon being withdrawn. Due to how taxes work for children, it is typical for parents to open the Roth, since child income is generally lower and they can benefit from the longer time horizon for tax free growth. The IRA can be invested in any way one sees fit for their situation including stocks, bonds, mutual funds, etc.

Another consideration at this point, is college planning. The process for financial aid should start now if one hasn't already done so. Because financial aid looks back two years, it's encouraged to begin to review if accounts are held in a student's name. Also, parental assets should be looked at as well to make sure they are set up efficiently. Custodian accounts carry more weight in the Expected Family Contribution formula, the financial aid calculation, called the EFC calculation, so families tend to move them, either to a custodial 529 account or use the assets for other things. One has to be careful of liquidating any investment due to tax considerations but it might make sense depending on the financial aid impact. Do the comparison of tax liability versus potential aid to determine the right plan of action.

AGE 16 COLLEGE PLANNING

————————————

Currently, the financial aid forms the government uses to determine aid eligibility is called the FAFSA Form, Free Application For Financial Student Aid. The information used to determine eligibility uses income from the two previous year's tax returns. For planning purposes, it's encouraged to review and start planning for where you have assets and the interest and dividend income you receive before you file this form. Review things such as assets that are in the child's name. Look at assets that are in the family name that could be used for college, such as savings accounts, money markets and non-qualified brokerage accounts. They're added into the aid equation. If possible, look at income in those years before filing as well if you can.

AGE 18 AGE OF MAJORITY — TAKE OVER CUSTODIAN ACCOUNTS

Once a child reaches age of majority, 18 or 21 depending on state UTMA, UGMA laws, the minor now can take over the accounts into their name. Obviously, this poses some interesting discussions. From a planning perspective, it's a good opportunity to educate the child about the importance of saving and investing. Hopefully, the child will use the account to his or her benefit. It takes proper education and planning. Parents who consider gifting money over to kids or grandkids must think about children having access to potentially a large sum of money. Obviously, the parent or grandparent wouldn't want the money spent frivolously. Parents can consider a trust such as a minor's trust which controls the assets while the child is growing up so to speak. It can be paid out at designated ages, such as 18 to pay for school or age 25 for weddings or home purchase or even later in life when a person is typically more responsible.

AGE 22 FIRST JOB — SAVE FOR RETIREMENT

Everyone knows that saving early is the best way to start saving for retirement. The calculations are quite eye opening of the difference it takes to reach a retirement goal if one starts at age 20 versus 30 versus 40 and so on. The old saying of pay yourself first still rings true. The first thing a person should do once they get a job is set up their retirement savings account. For example, if one starts saving at age 20, $538 per month towards retirement, they will have a million dollars saved by age 60 assuming a 6 percent rate of return. Compare that with a person starting to save at 40, the amount needed to reach a million dollars by 60 is $2,265 per month, assuming a 6% rate of return.

If the company offers a matching contribution, it is advisable to contribute at least up to the match, its free money!! It will go a long way in the end to reaching your goal.

AGE 26 OUT FROM UNDER MOM AND DAD'S HEALTHCARE PLAN, BUDGETING

At age 26, you can no longer be under mom and dad's healthcare plan. You'll be either under a company healthcare plan or you will have to go out to buy health insurance on the exchanges.

If you've just started working, consider having a budget, it will help you keep track of spending, and keep you disciplined to saving and not spending wastefully. There are many resources and strategies out there. The first piece of advice is, pay yourself first. Set aside an amount in a retirement account through work or in an IRA. The second part of saving would be to put some aside in a savings account for an emergency fund. The emergency fund is typically thought of as six to twelve months of your expenses kept in a savings account or readily accessible account. If one loses a job or has to take disability, it might take that long to find a new job or to begin to receive benefits. In addition, you don't want to have to sell investments at an inopportune time when the markets might be down or have to create a potential adverse tax consequence. Then, split up your paycheck into buckets, setting aside money for each expense that must be paid. Hopefully, there is money left over to do things you'd like to do, either that cup of coffee in the morning or getting that pedicure once a month. If there isn't money left over, revisit your expenses and consider cutting them or working to reduce them. Guidelines are out there as rules of thumb as to how much should be for housing expenditures and for the other monthly expenditures. They're good guidelines because that's what banks will use if you want to qualify for a mortgage. Ratio's such as your debt-to-income ratio, meaning how much is your gross monthly income covers how much you spend on debts on your credit report. The ratio to target is 40% of your income going to your debts. That will help you qualify for a mortgage. Also, it will put you on track for a healthy financial plan. Speaking of mortgages, it's a good idea to check one's credit. It's worth it to set up a credit monitoring service as well. Of course, there are other ways to enhance one's credit, pay down debts such as credit cards, and to prepare for buying a house, find the one that works for you or work with a qualified professional such as an accountant or a financial planner to help.

AGE 30 FAMILY CONSIDERATIONS

By age 30, not always, but typical that people are into their lives. You might have a home and possibly have started a family. Common themes that arise at this point are life insurance, disability insurance, emergency fund, saving for college and retirement, maybe even caring for older parents. People start to think of all these things at this point, which becomes confusing for people to juggle life with good planning. It can be helpful to work with someone to begin to formulate a plan. It's a good idea to have some form of life insurance and disability insurance to cover a catastrophic situation. Aside from an emergency fund, insurance is the base of solid financial plan. The reason is if something were to happen, the rest of your investments and savings could be wiped out, ruining well thought out plans. As we said earlier, an emergency fund is typically thought of as six to twelve months of your expenses kept in a savings account. If one loses a job or has to take disability, it might take that long to find a new job or to begin to receive benefits.

Disability insurance is typically obtained through your job or you can buy it through an insurance company and it's usually reasonable. Pricing is based upon the riskiness of your work and your income.

AGE 40 RETIREMENT SAVING, COLLEGE PLANNING

40! Talk about pressure. At this time, multiple goals might take competing priorities such as saving for your retirement, and if one has kids, how to save for college and caring for aging parents. A common rule of thumb is to make sure one's retirement is solidified and on track before saving for college. The thought process here is that kids can get scholarships, grants, take loans, etc. They have a longer time horizon to pay off loans whereas retirement is coming soon, and you don't have the time horizon that the kids have. You can always gift to the kids to pay off debts if you're in the right financial situation.

As has been referenced before, there are different type of accounts you can use to save for retirement.

They include company provided plans, Individual Retirement Arrangements, tax deferred annuities, life insurance, or maybe you want to invest in a business, real estate or other investments.

A company provided plan such as 401k, 403B or 457 plan will allow you to save through payroll. The money contributed to the plan is tax deferred. You might have a Roth component inside your 401k, 403b, SEP or SIMPLE which allows you to contribute on an after-tax basis, and that money will now grow tax free. You can contribute $22,500 from your paycheck in 2023.

An IRA is another way to save for retirement on a pre-tax basis. You can save money in a Roth IRA on money that has already been taxed, called after tax monies. The amount that you can contribute is $6,500 per year if you are under age 50. The Roth IRA has income limits for contributions. The 2023 income phaseouts are $138,000 to $153,000 for single filers and $218,000 to $228,000 for married filing jointly.

You can also contribute to both an IRA and a company retirement plan if you're an active participant if your income is under certain limits. For 2023, the limits are $73,000 to $83,000 for a single filer and $116,000 to $136,000 if your married filing jointly. If your married filing separately, then the income limit is $0-$10,000. If you're not an active participant in a plan and are married to an active participant, then the income phaseout is $218,000 to $228,000 for the 2023 tax year. An IRA is an account set up on an individual basis, there is no joint retirement IRA, which is a common question.

Small businesses are eligible for other types of retirement plan's such as SEP IRA's, SIMPLE

IRA's or defined benefit pension plans. The contribution limit for a SIMPLE IRA in 2023 is $15,500. If your over 50, you can contribute an additional $3,500 to your SIMPLE IRA plan.

We've gone over college savings plans in previous chapters, but we'll review them again if your age 40 or older given your priorities. Refer to Age 16 for more information on college planning.

If saving for college, the most popular account is called a 529 college savings account. There are also prepaid savings plan, Coverdell Education Savings accounts or custodian accounts. There are differences and pros and cons of each account. The 529 plan, prepaid savings plan and Coverdell accounts have tax and financial aid benefits. They are typically weighted less in the Expected Family Contribution, which is the calculation used to determine financial aid. The custodian account is a bit more flexible in the sense they can be withdrawn at any time and used for any expenses. The money placed in that account is an irrevocable gift to the child and reverts to the child at age of majority, typically age 18 or 21, depending on the rules of your state.

You can use up to a lifetime maximum of $10,000 in a 529 plan to pay for qualified student loans. An additional $10,000 can be used to pay for each sibling, children, grandchildren or spouses.

Starting in 2024, the new SECURE Act now allows for a transfer from a 529 college savings plan to be moved to a Roth IRA. Often people ask what they can do with funds that are not used for college. The stipulations are the plan must have been established for at least 15 years.

Contributions and earnings on those contributions cannot be rolled over to the Roth IRA. The Roth must be in the name of the beneficiary of the 529 plan. The annual amount that can be rolled over is the annual contribution limit of the Roth IRA. This rollover counts as a contribution for the regular annual contribution so you cannot exceed the annual contribution limit when you combine the rollover of 529 assets and a regular contribution. The lifetime maximum rollover contribution is $35,000.

There are accounts that can be set up for disabled children. They are called ABLE accounts. Typically, when someone is receiving federal benefits, they're only allowed to have a certain level of income or assets. The planning to get around this was to use a Supplemental Needs trust. This allowed for the holding of the assets and the person would still be allowed their benefits. The ABLE account alleviates the need for the trust and makes it easier and more cost effective. An ABLE account is a tax advantaged account set up for individuals that were disabled before the age of 26. In 2026, ABLE accounts can be set up for someone that was disabled prior to age 46. The contributions grow tax free. The contribution limit for 2023 is the annual gift exclusion and it is $17,000. If the proceeds are used for expenses such as housing, education, transportation, training, personal support services, health, financial management and administrative services, legal fees, funeral and burial expenses, then they will grow tax free.

The beneficiary can contribute to the ABLE account if they have earned income. This can be above the annual gift exclusion. The contribution is limited to the lesser of the beneficiary's compensation or the poverty line for a one-person household. The poverty line for a one-person household is $13,590 and $27,750 for a family of four for 2023. If the beneficiary is covered by an employer retirement plan, and their employer contributes then they are unable to contribute to the ABLE account.

AGE 50 RETIREMENT CONTRIBUTIONS INCREASE

At age 50, the rules want to help savers for retirement by allowing more money to go into their accounts. It's called a catch-up provision and it applies to both IRA's and Qualified Retirement Plans such as 401k's. The catch up means that you can add more money to your accounts per year because you are over the age of 50. For example, you can add $6,500 currently to an IRA per year. When your 50, you can increase that by $1,000 so the total contribution is $7,500 per year. For a retirement plan through an employer, such as a 401k, the increase is $7,500. The current year 2023 contribution limit is $22,500 per year. Tack on the extra catch up, and someone 50 or older could add $30,000 to their plans. It's a powerful way to catch up your retirement savings.

Again, as we have said before, you can increase your SIMPLE IRA contribution by $3,500 per year at age 50 for the year 2023, for a total contribution about of $19,000.

The annual catch-up amount has now been indexed for inflation. Starting in 2024, there are new rules for the catch-up contributions in 401k's, 403b's and 457 plans. If your previous years wages were above $145,000, then the catch-up contribution must go to the Roth side of those plans. The annual wages will be adjusted for inflation. This will not be the case for IRA catch-up contributions.

The SECURE Act 2.0 has expanded the penalty free withdrawal on qualified plans at age 50 for Public Safety Workers. The penalty free withdrawal now includes private sector firefighters provided they separated from service in the year they turn 59 ½. The penalty free withdrawal includes Public Safety Worker exceptions for those under 50 if they performed 25 or more years of service for the employer sponsoring the plan. They must work for the same employer.

AGE 55 EARLY WITHDRAWAL FROM 401K, INCREASE IN HSA CONTRIBUTIONS

If you work for a company, and you have a 401k retirement plan, the rule of 55 comes into play. This means, that if you leave your job at age 55 or after, you will not have to pay an IRS imposed penalty when you take money out. The penalty is 10% of the withdrawal. One would still have to pay taxes on the money but it saves the penalty. Unless the plan options are less than desirable, it is typically common practice to keep the money in the retirement account until at 59 ½.

At age 55, your eligible for the Health Savings Account catch up contribution of $1,000. A Health Savings Account is a tax advantaged account, used for medical expenses later in life. Think of it as a retirement account for medical expenses. It allows you to contribute on a pre-tax basis, earnings grow tax free, and your distributions are tax free if used for qualified healthcare and medical expenses after age 65.

You're allowed a once in a lifetime rollover from your retirement account to your Health Savings Account. The maximum amount is the maximum annual contribution limit. In 2023, it's $3,850 per year for an individual and $7,750 for a family. You can rollover from a Roth or a Traditional IRA, it's probably best to move from a Traditional IRA, given the tax nature of the IRA being tax deferred and HSA's are tax free. In order to move your retirement account, you must be eligible for the HSA for 12 months following the move into the HSA. You can rollover money from a Qualified Retirement Plan such as a 401k or a 403b, then you can move to the HSA. Just make sure you're considering all your options and that it makes financial sense.

AGE 59 ½ PENALTY FREE WITHDRAWALS FROM RETIREMENT ACCOUNTS

Hurray! You've made it to an important age in retirement planning. At 59½, your now allowed to withdraw from all retirement accounts, including annuities, without the IRS imposed 10% penalty. Also, if you have started a withdrawal from your retirement accounts under a rule called 72(t), which allows for a distribution without a 10% penalty, then it can be stopped this year. As long as you have satisfied the 5-year time frame for withdrawals.

Another strategy you can access at 59½, is a Net Unrealized Appreciation transaction. It is a transaction where you can take out employer stock out of your retirement plan and have the gain on the stock treated as capital gain. Be careful though, it is a complex transaction but could help save on future taxes. As with all planning strategies, it is best to check with a tax or financial professional to see if it appropriate for your situation.

AGE 60 SOCIAL SECURITY AGE FOR WIDOW

Starting at age 60, if you are a widow, you're allowed to start taking Social Security. The widower can receive benefits at any age when there are eligible children. Eligible children are under the age of 16 or disabled. The amount of the benefit is determined by earnings. The family can receive benefits as well, as long as the children are under age 18 or disabled before age 22. In order to qualify for survivor benefits, the survivor must be married for at least nine months before death occurs, unless military or due to accident, no time requirement. Must also be parent of children for children to receive benefits. A disabled widower between age 50-59 may also qualify for benefits.

AGE 60 RETIREMENT IS ON THE HORIZON, ADDITION CATCH-UP CONTRIBUTIONS IN 2024

Hopefully, by age 60, you've done your homework and prepared for retirement. It's not the worst thing in the world to start late but it makes things more difficult. If you've arrived at 60 and don't have anything saved, hopefully you can still work and save. Make budget or spending plan, save and take advantage of anything you can to build a nest egg you can live off. You'll also have Social Security and it's a good idea to check how much you'll receive. You can go onto SSA.gov to create your log on and check your benefits. You'll have Medicare or Medicaid to help you for healthcare costs as well. There are other programs to assist people with food, housing and medical. Hopefully you won't have to rely on them, and you can continue to work and save for retirement. You can continue to add to retirement accounts as long as you keep working.

Starting in 2025, 401k's and 403b's and SIMPLE IRA's will have a higher catch-up contribution. Participants will have a catch-up contribution at age 60, 61, 62 and 63. The amount will be the greater of $10,000 or 150% of the regular catch-up contribution for plan years 2024 for 401k's and 403b's. SIMPLE IRA's will have a $5,000 catch-up increase or 150% of the regular SIMPLE catch-up amount for 2025, whichever is greater.

AGE 62 ELIGIBLE FOR SOCIAL SECURITY

At age 62, you're now eligible to receive your Social Security payment. Just bear in mind, at this age you're allowed only 75% of your full payment because it's an early payment. From a planning standpoint, it's usually recommended to only take it early if you need the money. If you don't take it, your payment will grow on average 8% per year until age 70. If longevity is in your family, and you expect to live longer, you will make more out of the system if the payment is left to grow, especially the longer one lives. There is debate as to when to take it and how to take it if your single or married. Work with a professional to determine the best course of action.

AGE 63 MEDICARE PART B AWARENESS

If you are planning on taking Medicare at age 65, you'll have two parts, Part A and Part B. Part A is paid for by the government. We pay for Part B out of Social Security payments. The payment is a tier system based upon income. The income they use to determine your payment is based on your income from two years prior. The issue becomes if you were working at age 63 but are retired at age 65. Your income is most likely lower yet you're paying premiums based on the higher income. The premium for 2023 starts at $164.90 but can go as high as $560.50 per month. The income tiers will now start to be indexed for inflation, but it starts with the lower income brackets first and the higher brackets won't be increased until 2028. For 2023, the first tier starts at Modified Adjusted Gross Income of $97,000 from 2021 for a single filer. If married filing joint, if your Modified Adjusted Gross Income in 2021 was $194,000 or higher, you start to pay higher Medicare Premiums. The highest tier starts at Modified Adjusted Gross Income of $500,000 for single filers and $750,000 for joint filers. Your 2023 part B deductible is $226 before you start to pay out of pocket.

Medicare Part D also has an Income Related Monthly Adjustment Amount. Medicare Part D is your prescription drug plan. The income brackets are the same as Part B. If your Modified Adjusted Gross income is below the first threshold, $97,000 filing single in 2021 or $194,000 filing joint, then the premium is the plan premium. The highest premium in 2023 is your plan premium plus $76.40 per month.

How to plan for this issue? The first is being aware of the issue. The second is to shelter as much income as possible in those years before eligibility. Things such as adding to retirement accounts and take advantage of catch ups. Also, during retirement, your income matters so getting money into tax advantaged accounts such as Roth IRA's or Health Savings Accounts. If you own a business, then being aware of tax rules and maximize all deductions and credits. Also, at 70½, you can do a Qualified Charitable Distribution which can reduce your taxable income.

Sometimes, the above things are not possible, or you want to take advantage of the above but also inform the government of your income change. You can file form SSA-44. This will allow you to inform them of your change in status and your now lowered income which will help you lower your Medicare premiums.

AGE 65 MEDICARE ELIGIBLE AGE, HEALTH SAVINGS ACCOUNTS POTENTIALLY STOP

At age 65, you're allowed to sign up for Medicare. If you currently have healthcare provided by an employer, then Medicare becomes the secondary provider. If not, then signing up is urged. The reason is that every year that passes, Medicare assesses a penalty which increases your premiums. If you're on a company's plan, consider the cost implications in deciding whether to sign up for a plan. You also have a decision of whether to sign up for Medicare and buy a supplemental plan called a Medigap plan, or whether to buy a Medicare Advantage plan. The needs are typically based on what expenses you're currently using or would want covered.

At age 65, and if you're signing up for Medicare, you are no longer able to contribute to a Health

Savings Account. If you continue to work and are under a High Deductible Plan, you may be able to contribute to the plan, but the rules get tricky so it's best to review the rules and your situation. Distributions before age 65 and not used for a qualified medical expense carry a 20% penalty. At age 65, you can use the money in the account for non-medical expenses and avoid a 20% penalty, you only have to pay taxes. Distributions from HSA's for qualified medical expenses are tax free. The distributions can be for you, your spouse or your dependents. You are allowed to contribute to the account if your enrolled in a High Deductible Health Plan. In 2023, you're allowed to contribute $3,850 between you and your employer as individual coverage or $7,750 for family coverage. The High Deductible Health Plan minimums are $1,500 for an Individual and $3,000 for a family.

The High Deductible Health Plan maximum out of pocket is $7,500 for Individuals and $15,000 for a family, this includes deductibles, co-pays, other amounts. Premiums are not included in the above amount.

AGE 66 NORMAL RETIREMENT AGE

If you were born between the years 1943 and 1954, then your normal retirement age according to Social Security is age 66. If you were born in 1955, then your normal retirement for Social Security purposes is 66 and 2 months. If you were born in 1956, then your normal retirement age is 66 and 4 months. Each year add 2 months until you get to 1960. If you were born in 1960 or later, then normal retirement age is 67.

AGE 70 SOCIAL SECURITY AGE, QUALIFIED LONGEVITY CONTRACT, QUALIFIED CHARITABLE DISTRIBUTION AGE

Since you have attained the age of 70, Social Security benefits cease to grow at this point. So, there is no reason to wait. Make sure you file with the government to take your benefit. It is potentially taxable depending on your income limits and it can also increase the income tax rates on other income. Remember, if you have deferred your IRA distribution and your Social Security, your income typically increases this year so be prepared. Hopefully you have done your planning up until this point.

At age 70½, if you don't need the income from the IRA or would prefer to keep your taxes low, then there is an option that they government has come up with. You can now grant your distribution to charity. You can do what's called a Qualified Charitable Distribution, which allows you to distribute up to $100,000 per year to a qualified charity and not have it taxed. It's a nice way to help charity and save on taxes. The annual allowable amount is now indexed for inflation.

Another way to defer the distribution is to employ what's called a Qualified Longevity Annuity Contract. The government allowed this strategy because people are living longer and would prefer to have income for expenses later in life such as healthcare costs, etc. You can set this up at any age the insurance company allows. It allows you add a premium from your IRA or qualified retirement account up to $200,000 in 2023, to be carved off into an annuity. The balance is not counted towards the required distribution therefore it would reduce your required distribution and therefore taxable income. You can defer the distribution up to age 85 or any age in between. One strategy for using a Qualified Longevity Annuity Contract would be if a spouse passes away, that person's Social Security, if higher moves to the spouse, but the spouse loses their social security. If this is a concern, then the QLAC can be used to pick up the lost income from the spouse's Social Security going away.

AGE 73 REQUIRED DISTRIBUTION AGE

At this age, the government requires you to take a portion of your retirement savings accounts. The exception is a Roth IRA. Quite a few people have questions on how it works, how much to take and when does it have to start. The good thing is you only have to take a small portion out each year. If you've reached this point and haven't taken any, you probably don't need the money. We discussed ways to defer your withdrawal previously.

Up until this year, the required distribution was age 72. Late in 2022, the Secure Act 2.0 was passed, and it increased the Required Distribution age to age 73. If you turned 72 in 2023, then you have another year before you have to take your distribution. It will gradually increase to age 75 in

2033. To summarize, if you were born in 1950 or before, your distribution will be age 72. If you were born in 1951 to 1959, your required distribution age is 73. If you were born in 1960 or later, your new required distribution age is 75.

You are required to take your mandatory required distribution by April 1st of the year after you turn 73. The calculation is based on the previous year's December 31st ending balance and an IRS provided Uniform Lifetime Expectancy Table. If your spouse is the sole beneficiary and is more than 10 years younger, you can use the Joint Life Expectancy Table. The balance in the account is divided by the life expectancy number given in the table.

You might be thinking, well life expectancy goes down every year, does the distribution change? Sure, the account balance changes but also life expectancy decreases. Each year, your life expectancy declines so the ratio or percentage withdrawn goes up. The idea is to reduce the balance in the account to zero. The IRS wants their taxes on this money since you received a benefit when it went in, so they want their benefit back!

This distribution ruling applies to retirement accounts including Traditional IRA's, 401k's, 403b's and Employer Provided Tax Shelter Annuity or TSA's, 457 plans, SIMPLE IRA's, SEP IRA's, Profit Sharing Plans, and other defined contribution plans, etc. You get the point. Everything except Roth IRA's or Non-qualified annuities. Annuities have their own set of rules set by the insurance company.

However, if you are still working, and not over a 5% owner of the company, you can defer the required distribution in your qualified retirement plans. Oftentimes I see people rolling over IRA's back over to their qualified retirement plans to avoid the distribution.

Sometimes, a question arises, can you take from one account and not another. In some case's the answer is yes. In order to figure out the Required Minimum Distribution at the end of the year, you take all of your IRA's and add them up and divide by the appropriate life expectancy factor. For the other plans, each plan tends to require you to take the distribution from their plan. For example, if you have two 401k's, the providers will require you to take the distribution from each plan. If you have two 403b's, the providers might allow you to aggregate the plans and take from one or other. Best advice, check with your plan's providers.

There are other questions that often come up. Such as, can the distribution from the account be put back into a retirement account or converted over to a Roth? Also, can someone continue to contribute to IRA's or retirement plans after 73? Good questions. The required distribution must be taken out and stay out of a retirement account for the most part. The determining factor as to whether you can add to a retirement account is having earned income. So, if you are 73, and are forced to take a distribution but you or a spouse has earned income, then you can contribute. Each person's situation is different, obviously check with your tax professional. If someone is still working, they can defer the distribution in a company retirement account if they are not more than 5 % owner of the company.

Another issue to be aware of is the timing or coordinating your distribution if you're doing a Qualified Charitable Distribution. You need to take your Qualified Charitable Distribution first, then take out any additional required amounts afterwards. For example, supposed you had a calculated distribution of $10,000 for the year. You decided to give $5,000 to charity. That amount must come out first. Then, the remaining amount comes out afterwards. Your custodian typically has a form to handle the charitable distribution.

When you take your distribution, you have several options as to when it comes out. You can ask for your distribution at any time. Your distribution can be one time during the year, say the end of the year, beginning of the year, on your birthday or other day you might need it such as property tax time. You can have the distribution come out automatically, say once a month or once per year on a specified day. If you're taking your distribution from an IRA, you can choose how much in taxes to be withheld. Your state might have a withholding requirement. If you are taking from a qualified plan such as a 401k or 403b, they will have a mandatory withholding of 20% for federal taxes and your state could require some to be withheld. You can certainly withhold more. The distribution can be sent to your bank, or a check can be sent by mail.

ROTH CONVERSIONS

Let's say, you wanted to move some of your money to a Roth IRA. It's called a Roth Conversion. One might ask, can you convert the Required Distribution. Again, the required distribution must come out of the retirement account. Anything above the Required Distribution can be converted over to a ROTH IRA.

Phew! Hopefully that clears up the distribution questions somewhat.

What if you miss a distribution? It happens, and the penalty is steep at 25% of what was supposed to be distributed. It goes down to 10% if your shortfall is corrected within a specified window. This "Correction Window" begins on the date the tax penalty is imposed which is the first day of the following year you were required to take out the distribution. The window ends on the earliest of the day a Notice of Delinquency was mailed, when the tax was assessed by the IRS, or the last day of the second tax year after the tax is imposed. You can request a waiver of the penalty however it's important to withdraw the missed amount because it must come out.

Another consideration when age 73, and you have a 401(k) plan with a Roth side to it. If you don't need the money, then rolling over the plan assets to a Roth IRA will help you keep the Roth growing tax free until a later date. If one keeps the money inside the 401(k), then the distribution is composed partly of pre-tax contributions and a proportional distribution will come out of the Roth. You have more control over the account if it's in your name and split between the two types of accounts.

This will change in 2024 when the Roth component of qualified plans will essentially match the rules of the Roth IRA, and there will be no required distribution.

AGE 85 FORCED WITHDRAWAL ON QLAC

_____

Recently, the IRS updated rules on the Required Distribution on retirement accounts. They have allowed for a portion of a person's retirement accounts to be deferred in order to allow for income later in life. At age 85, the Qualified Longevity Annuity must begin payout.

AGE 90 TYPICAL ANNUITY COMMENCEMENT DATE

If one has an annuity that is not an IRA, annuity companies will have an age that stipulates when the money must start being withdrawn. The ages differ per company and contract but tend to start around age 90. Given longer lifespans, they are increasing the ages but be aware of contract rules. The withdrawal can be in form of annuitization, lump sum or reoccurring withdrawal.

INHERITING AN IRA

What happens if someone passes away with an IRA account? The answer depends on the titling of the accounts and who, if any are the beneficiaries on an account.

Let's say that you have an IRA with designated beneficiaries, say a spouse. The spouse has the option of rolling over the account into their own name. Most times this is the preferred way to go for simplicity and ease of management. Another way is a spouse can keep the account in an Inherited IRA. This tends to become the case if the spouse beneficiary is under the age of 59 ½ and needs to access the funds without penalty. A withdrawal can be made without a 10% penalty, otherwise, if the spouse is under 59 ½, and they move it to their own name, they will be accessed a penalty. A withdrawal on a non-Roth IRA is considered taxable income to the beneficiary.

The Inherited Roth IRA earnings are taxable if the Roth wasn't opened for 5 years.

If the inheritor is an eligible designated beneficiary such a surviving spouse, minor child, chronically ill or disabled person, or beneficiary not more than 10 years younger than the owner, then the distribution will be over the life expectancy of the inheritor. Once the minor child reaches the age of majority, the account must be distributed according to the ten- year time frame unless the child is pursuing an education and thus they can be granted an extension on the 10-year rule up to age 26.

If the spouse is the only beneficiary, they can elect to be treated as the deceased spouse. This new rule begins in 2024 and allows for an older spouse to use the deceased spouses age to determine Required Minimum Distributions. The older spouse can use the Uniform Lifetime Table instead of the Single Life Table for beneficiaries. If the surviving spouse dies, and required distributions have not begun, then the beneficiaries would be treated as the original beneficiary of the account. They wouldn't be subject to the 10-year rule, they would be able to use their life expectancy for calculating the distribution.

If someone inherits an IRA, qualified plan or Inherited IRA after 2020, and they are a non-spouse beneficiary, 10 years or younger than the original owner, then they must distribute the entire account by the end of the 10th year following the owner's death.

If the original owner of the IRA was taking

required distributions, the designated beneficiary must take out the minimum distribution according to the same schedule the owner was taking their distributions. Then, they must have the account depleted by the end of the 10th year after the year of death of the owner.

If the IRA does not have a beneficiary, then the account must be distributed within 5 years of passing.

AGE BASED INVESTING

As you can see, attainment of a certain age determines a lot of the planning we discuss with people. There are age-based investments called Target Date Funds. Most times they are used for retirement or retirement distribution. You'll notice them by having a year in the name of the fund. Such as Target 2025 or Target 2060 fund. The year of the fund coincides with the year someone is retiring. They invest the funds according to that time horizon. They have a glide path and slowly get more conservative as the date nears. They continue to operate after the target date and eventually get to a conservative mix a number of years after the target date. Some funds stay around for ten years after the target date and then fold into another fund designed for retirees. The fund that it's folded into has a conservative mix.

There are other variations on the target date funds such as Target Risk funds, designed to hold a particular risk level. There are also funds that will create an income stream all within one fund. Also, in bond funds, they have something called bullet shares, where all the bonds mature in a particular year. This helps alleviate interest rate risk.

The benefits of a Target Date fund are that they are simple, little to no minimum, professionally managed and cost effective. The fund will do all the investing in the major asset classes. It will also rebalance back to the appropriate asset mix.

The disadvantage with the funds is that they aren't tailored to the investor. They tend to have broad retirement years in terms of the options. Options are laid out as years, but you'll see them in five-year increments. If you're retiring in a year that is between the five-year increment, it might not be the best option in terms of risk. Also, it doesn't know you as an investor, you might be an aggressive investor or a more conservative investor. The fund doesn't know your situation, you might want growth funds or dividend funds to achieve your particular goal. You might also be interested in a certain attributes such as ESG investing, which are screened for environmental, social or governance factors that align to your wishes. Also, they are made up of actively managed funds or passive funds, you might or might not want that. In addition, they are created from one provider, so the underlying funds or investments are made up of that carrier's funds. You might want to create a portfolio of various managers depending on their skill or area of expertise.

Also, you might want to use other vehicles such as exchange traded funds or individual stocks, bond or alternatives such as real estate or private investments.

The other issue is control and taxes. If you want to control the underlying parts to either overweight or underweight a certain asset class or sector, it's impossible to have that done within the fund. Also, the funds can have tax efficient investments inside the fund itself, such as index funds but they don't have the option to have additional tax managed benefits such as tax loss harvesting and other tax smart techniques such as tax-free bonds.

FINAL THOUGHTS

I hope that you found the information in this guide helpful. It was designed to be a roadmap to use throughout life and to answer common planning questions. As you can imagine, rules change so you should always check back on the most current rules and laws. In addition, you should work with a qualified professional to make sure that you're doing the right thing for your situation.

Printed in the United States
by Baker & Taylor Publisher Services